Why Me?

Tim Dieffenbach

when life's not fair

FAITH ALIVE®
Christian Resources

Grand Rapids, Michigan

We are grateful to Tim Dieffenbach for writing this course. Tim is Minister of Parish Life at Central Reformed Church, Grand Rapids, Michigan.

Faith Alive Christian Resources published by CRC Publications.

We welcome your comments. Call us at 1-800-333-8300 or e-mail us at editors@faithaliveresources.org.

ISBN 1-56212-787-X

Contents

Introduction

Life for today's young people is increasingly complex and confusing. Through this series, we want to help high school youth find a basic frame of reference for living in this sometimes-difficult world. By inviting teens to express their faith openly and actively, both in word and in deed, we can help them become a positive force for change in their complex world of work, school, and society.

Our goals for this series are as follows:

- to promote a healthy discussion of life issues
- to develop a biblical and Reformed perspective on life issues
- to make choices that are rooted in God's Word
- to grow in our personal commitment to live as God's people in a secular culture

Why Me? When Life's Not Fair is part of the LifeWise series for high school youth. Each course in the series offers four sessions dedicated to issues that are important to young people. Each book includes step-by-step instructions for leading group meetings and handouts that may be photocopied for students' use.

These courses are intended to create a forum for discussion of important issues. You, as group leader, will be facilitating that discussion as together your group addresses different problems. You will encourage group members to think critically about where they stand personally in relation to these issues and about how their Christian life affects the way they act and live on a day-to-day basis.

GOALS AND CONTENT

The goals of *Why Me? When Life's Not Fair* are as follows:

- to provide a safe place to reflect about our "loss experiences" and explore our feelings toward God, others, and ourselves during these times
- to examine our thoughts about the nature of God as we face suffering and loss

- to discuss the losses families experience during divorce, and to find ways to care for those whose families are going through divorce
- to explore our thoughts about death and dying and the grieving process
- to consider a Christian response to tragedy in our own lives and the lives of others

The four meetings of this course deal with the following themes:

- Meeting 1 sets the stage for the three remaining sessions. It raises the question "When has life not treated you fairly?" We'll look at two biblical sufferers (Job and Jesus), explore two case studies of Christians who have opposing views on death, and consider God's fairness versus our faithfulness as we reflect on our losses.
- Meeting 2 takes an honest look at the impact of divorce on family members, especially adolescents. We'll complete a Bible study on God's intentions for marriage, then look at how to survive a divorce in the family and how to help others in that situation. We'll explore the separation and loss of divorce, but we'll also see how the principles of healing and forgiveness can bring hope and provide for new beginnings.
- Meeting 3 focuses on loss as it relates to death. We will all die, and we all know people who have died. Unfortunately we usually avoid talking about dying and death. In this session we'll demystify the subject of death, look at the Bible's perspective, and identify some myths and truths about the grieving process.
- Meeting 4 focuses on loss when sudden tragedy strikes. We'll look at tragedies in the news and ask ourselves how we would respond if we were the ones involved. We'll explore Bible passages that offer practical advice and point us toward hope and trust in God. Finally, we'll learn how to become involved in a "ministry of presence" to hurting people.

MATERIALS

To lead the course you'll need this book. You'll want to photocopy the handouts at the back of this book for yourself and for each group member. The meeting guides and handouts are explained in more detail below.

You'll also need Bibles, paper, pencils or pens, markers, and a pad of newsprint or other large sheets of paper. Check the *Materials* list of each meeting for any other items you'll need to lead the session.

AUDIENCE AND GENERAL APPROACH

This course is designed for four discussion-based meetings and is intended for use by high school youth. It can be used in church school, youth group, or retreat settings.

Ideally you should have a full hour for each of the four meetings. You'll find there are plenty of activities to fill sixty minutes or more. Should you have less time, you'll need to trim or even omit some suggested steps. But be sure not to settle for less than forty-five minutes per meeting.

This course uses many small group activities. They're lively and fun, and they help participants learn from each other. They are designed to encourage participants to delve into each issue, to think deeply about how each issue affects their lives, and to discuss each issue from a Christian perspective.

LEADER'S ROLE

As leader, your main tasks are the following:

- to get to know each group member
- to keep the various activities moving and on track
- to facilitate discussion and interaction
- to model what it means to be open to God's Word and Spirit

Try to cultivate an atmosphere of openness that allows each person to feel free and secure. Think of yourself as a colearner with the group, a fellow traveler on a journey of faith.

To prepare for each meeting, carefully read through the meeting guide material. This material is explained for you below.

USING LIFEWISE

The meeting guides will help you prepare for and lead the meetings. They will tell you when and how to use the handouts at the back of this book.

Scripture
Here you'll find the Scripture passages used during the meeting.

Today's Theme
This brief introductory section is intended to start you thinking about the day's theme and what the issue at hand means for your group.

Goals of the Meeting
Each meeting plan provides a set of goals that you can refer to throughout your meeting time to keep your discussion on track. These goals should constitute a guideline for your meeting, not a strict rule. We encourage you to add goals as needed to fit the needs and interests of the teens in your group.

Materials
This section lists all the materials you'll need for the meeting, including any materials you'll need for warm-up group activities.

Theme Thoughts
This section is designed to give you, as leader, a deeper biblical/theological perspective on the issue you're addressing in the meeting. Please resist any impulse to lecture to the group on this section's contents. It's just for you.

Meeting Plan (Steps)
Different every meeting, these steps are designed to give you interesting and "active" methods for reaching the goals of the meeting. Some of these steps use the handouts, others do not.

Variations
Some of the steps conclude with "variations" or ways to adapt a particular step to the learning styles of group members, to the size of your group, or to the materials you have available.

Options
These optional activities are intended to increase your flexibility in leading your group and to stimulate your creativity. Substitute these steps for others in the meeting plan when and if you feel that the option would be more meaningful or appealing to your group members.

Handouts
All handouts are included at the back of this book. Prior to each meeting time, photocopy the necessary handouts and have them ready to distribute at the appropriate time.

The handouts are used during the meetings for a variety of activities. They contain prompts for biblical study, group activities, surveys, and other material. Handouts are numbered sequentially throughout the course.

ADDITIONAL SUGGESTIONS FOR LEADERS

Be personal!
First, be personal in the sense of being yourself. Don't try to be something you normally aren't. Most teens can immediately see through an adult who is trying to be "cool" just to impress them. Be yourself, and act your age.

Second, be personal in the sense that you respect each young person for who he or she is, for the strength of his or her character, and for the ability to reason and apply what he or she is learning through these meetings.

Third, be personal in the way you see yourself: as a leader but also as a colearner with the group. Let them know you don't have all the answers, that you are on a faith journey *with* them.

Don't be afraid to say "I don't know" or "I'm not sure" or "Help me think that through, will you?" Applying our Christian principles to issues can be difficult and perplexing—for adults as well as for young people.

Be a good listener!
Resist the temptation to do all of the talking yourself (otherwise known as lecturing). Learn to be a good listener, even if it means patiently enduring times of silence. Give group members time to think and to respond. Show by your comments and your body language that you appreciate their contributions (even if you don't agree with everything they say).

When you do ask questions, remember to keep a good balance of questions of fact, questions of opinion or interpretation, and questions of foundations. The last category of questions asks people to explain the basis on which they have made their judgments. An important part of your task is to help your group recognize the value of basing their judgments on Scripture and on the teachings of the church.

Look for and take advantage of opportunities for your group members to take responsibility for the meeting's activities. In doing so you'll provide them with a sense of ownership for the group discussion and activities.

Be creative!
Use this material to guide—not dictate—your meetings. Adapting the discussion topics and activities to better suit your situation should be your goal as a group leader. We offer variations on individual steps and some alternative steps (at the end of each meeting plan) to allow you more flexibility and choice in leading your meetings.

You may find that each meeting has more material in it than you can cover in the time you have available. Feel free to pick and choose between the steps, the options at the end of the meeting plan, and your own ideas. Make it *your* meeting, tailored to the needs and interests of *your* group.

Have fun!
Learning is meant to be enjoyable. We are called to enjoy God and to celebrate God's goodness. Reflect that celebration in your setting. If you are confined to a room at church, avoid placing the chairs in an arrangement that looks and feels like school. Use the

games and other exercises not only to learn together but also to laugh together.

Videos
Leaders interested in supplementing this course with age-appropriate videos on divorce, death and dying, grieving, and suffering are invited to contact to TRAVARCA, the film and video library of the Christian Reformed Church in North America and the Reformed Church in America. For information on services provided by TRAVARCA, call 1-800-968-7221 or e-mail travarca@iserv.net.

EVALUATION FORMS

At the end of this book are a leader's evaluation form for you to complete and an evaluation form for group members that you may photocopy and distribute. You can help us improve this series by completing these forms.

Please send completed evaluation forms to

LifeWise
Faith Alive Christian Resources
2850 Kalamazoo Ave. SE
Grand Rapids, Michigan 49560

The "Why" Question

Summary of the book of Job; Mark 14:32-36; 15:22-39

TODAY'S THEME

The church does teenagers a disservice when it offers them simplistic answers to complicated questions about their faith and about how to integrate their faith into real life responses. Simplistic answers may offer an easy way out, but they only add to the doubt and confusion teens are already feeling.

Imagine Brett, age sixteen. When he asks a church member why God allowed his father to die, he gets this response: "God must have needed him more than we did." What? God needs Brett's father more than Brett needs him? Now imagine Heather, age fifteen. When she tells her friends at church that her parents are going to divorce, her youth group leader says, "You may not be able to understand this now, but this is all part of God's plan for your life." Can it really be true that God's plan for a teenage girl's life is to rip apart the fabric of her family?

Young people deserve better care and more thought-filled responses when they ask tough questions like these. Of course, exploring these issues honestly is far more difficult than offering Christian platitudes. There are risks involved. We might not have all the "right" answers. Our own fear and lack of under-standing of complex issues may come to light. But what fertile ground for growth and maturity for leaders and teens alike!

In this first session, you should focus on making room for faith questions rather than providing an-swers. The reality of the Christian faith is that we don't have all the answers to life's circumstances. Paul reminds us in 1 Corinthians 13:12 that "now we see but a poor reflection as in a mirror; then we shall see face to face." Especially as teens strive to make sense out of life's hardships, we should provide for them a safe place to explore their fears about life and their questions about God. When they wonder where God is when tragedy strikes, when they feel aban-doned by God, we can assure them that they are in good company—the Bible is full of stories of God's people who doubted God's faithfulness.

GOALS OF THE MEETING

- to reflect on some of the hard questions about why bad things happen to us
- to discover what the stories of Job's suffering and Jesus' suffering can teach us about our own suffering and loss
- to identify two opposite explanations of suffering, and to articulate a personal response to suffering
- to redefine the "why" question with a "what" question

MATERIALS

1. Bibles
2. Handouts 1-6 (5 and 6 are optional), pens
3. Newsprint, marker
4. Agree/Disagree signs, as described in step 2
5. Masking tape

THEME THOUGHTS

From sharing our first toys with other toddlers to competing with peers for a spot on the basketball team or first chair in the school band, we expect life to be fair. So what happens when we play by the rules and still get burned?

Life seems unfair when we find it difficult to explain certain events or circumstances. Teens feel the press-ing realities of war, hunger, disease, school shoot-ings, natural disasters, and all the other tragedies they see on the evening news as their worldview expands. They struggle to find answers, especially when bad things happen to good people. All of us, whether we're young or old, want order in our lives, not chaos. We want life to be predictable. We feel more secure when there are answers to our questions. And when we face personal loss or tragedy, knowing the "right" answer seems even more important.

In some ways, our search for answers is a symptom of the human condition. We exercise a great deal of control over our lives. But when we are faced with a loss—whether it is the end of a romantic relationship or the death of a loved one—we realize we are not in control of everything. Sometimes we feel we are drowning in our own anger. Sometimes we doubt the security of our future or wrestle with thoughts of abandonment. We wonder if we are being punished for something we did or failed to do. Often we are forced to look for answers beyond our own actions and ourselves. We begin to rely on our faith to provide these answers. Whether we're looking for a scapegoat or for stability, we look to God.

C. S. Lewis put it bluntly:

Where is God? This is one of the most disquieting symptoms. When you are happy, so happy that you have no sense of needing Him, if you turn to Him then with your praise, you will be welcomed with open arms. But go to Him when your need is desperate, when all other help is vain and what do you find? A door slammed in your face, and a sound of bolting and double bolting on the inside. After that, silence. You may as well turn away.

—*A Grief Observed*, p. 9

Lewis was not alone in his feelings. As Job endured hardships, he wondered where God was: "I cry out to you, O God, but you do not answer; I stand up, but you merely look at me. You turn on me ruthlessly" (Job 30:20-21). And in the garden of Gethsemane, Jesus "plunged into a sinkhole of dreadful agony" and begged his Father, "You can—can't you?—get me out of this" (Mark 14:32-33, *The Message*). Later, on the cross, Jesus cried out, "My God, my God, why have you forsaken me?" (Matt. 27:46).

The truth is that we cannot understand life's "unfair" circumstances in terms of God's fairness. Fairness is a question that bears our own expectations of equality. Only by remaining faithful to God can we begin to receive the benefit of hope and healing when life seems unfair.

As a friend and former colleague once said, "God gets us out of nothing, but through everything."

1 WHERE IS GOD?

10 minutes

Distribute Handout 1 ("Where Is God?") and pens. Read this dramatic description aloud to the group. Use the questions on side 2 of the handout for discussion with the entire group.

Don't get into any lengthy discussion at this point; the object is mainly to introduce the topic and raise questions. If the group raises questions of their own (for example, in response to question 1), don't respond now. Simply write their questions on a piece of newsprint or white board and keep them available throughout the course. You'll refer to the list of questions again in meeting 4.

VARIATION

An optional approach is to have kids write out the answers to the questions on the handout, then discuss. This will take longer, of course, but should produce more thoughtful responses from more kids than the shorter version of the step.

2 IS GOD FAIR?

10 minutes

Distribute Handout 2 ("Is God Fair?") and read the directions to the group:

We believe that God is all-loving, all-powerful, and all-present, yet the fact remains that there is much suffering in the world. Read each of the following statements and circle the response that best expresses your view. Do not take a lot of time on each statement.

While kids are writing (or prior to class), make five signs, as follows, using markers and ordinary paper:

- totally agree
- somewhat agree
- neutral
- somewhat disagree
- totally disagree

Fasten the signs to the wall, beginning with "totally agree" in one corner and ending with "totally disagree" in an opposite corner. Go through the nine statements on Handout 2 and have the students move to the place in the room that best represents their personal views on each of the statements. For each statement, give a couple of students an opportunity to explain why they chose to stand where they did. Be sure to give a representative of opposing positions the chance to respond. Ask students who are standing in the "neutral" zone why they are undecided.

VARIATION

To save time (and eliminate photcopying Handout 2), simply read the statements aloud and have kids take their places along the agree/disagree scale. Read slowly and repeat each statement so kids have it clearly in mind before reacting.

3 TWO GREAT SUFFERERS: JOB AND JESUS

20 minutes

Distribute Handout 3 ("Two Great Sufferers: Job and Jesus"). Divide the class into two groups of two to five persons each, trying to get a balance of talkers and quieter teens in each group. If you have more than ten kids in your class, divide into three or four smaller groups.

Ask half of the small groups to read about Job and discuss the questions that follow the reading. Ask the other half to read about Jesus and discuss the questions that follow that reading. All groups should be ready to share their answers with the entire class.

Before the groups start to work, have them quickly choose kids to fill each of these roles (one teen can hold several roles, if needed):

- Reader (reads the story about Job and the Scripture about Jesus and all questions)
- Discussion starter (always responds first to each question)
- Timekeeper (keeps the group on task so they'll finish all the work in ten minutes)
- Presenter (presents the group's answers to the class)

If possible, let groups go to an area where they will not be distracted by other groups—in the hall, in a corner of a stairwell, in the church auditorium. Give them ten minutes to finish their work.

Have the small groups present their answers to the class (if more than one group has the same topic, divide the reporting between the groups).

When you talk about Job, focus on the reasons why God doesn't explain our suffering. Beuchner suggests that we wouldn't understand. And even if we did understand, it still wouldn't make the suffering go away. Maybe your group can add other reasons as well.

Also be sure your group understands that while God doesn't explain why we suffer, God doesn't abandon us to suffer alone either. "He reveals himself. He shows his face." God is with us when we suffer.

When you talk about Jesus, be sure to let the kids suggest ways that Jesus' suffering helps us endure our own suffering. You and the entire group may really be blessed by some of the responses you hear.

Focus on how the story of Jesus' suffering allows us to see that God is not removed from our suffering. God sent Jesus Christ to bear our sin; God suffered loss by offering his own Son for us. In Jesus, God identifies with our pain. The good news for us is the hope offered by the resurrection! It shows God's desire to provide wholeness and healing for a broken world. It's a love story that is filled with pain and challenge but also with healing and hope.

Be sure to ask if anyone has any additional questions or comments about either Job or Jesus and our own suffering. You may want to jot down more general questions on the sheet of newsprint.

VARIATION

If your kids don't work well in small groups, simply walk through Handout 3 with the entire group.

4 CASE STUDIES: TWO CHRISTIANS RESPOND TO LIFE LOSSES
15 minutes

Distribute Handout 6 ("Case Studies: Two Christians Respond to Life Loses"). Ask for volunteers to read the stories of Brian Sternberg and Jim Bowers aloud to the class. After the readings, discuss the two questions that follow:

- **What different responses to loss and suffering do Brian and Jim have?**

  Brian does not ask the "why" question, nor does he consider loss and suffering as part of God's divine plan. Instead he attempts to respond in faith to what has happened. On the other hand, Jim feels that loss and suffering are indeed part of God's divine plan. Jim's comfort is that he sees God's hand at work and knows God will use this suffering and loss to bring the good news of the gospel to others.

- **Is your own response to loss and suffering closer to Brian's or to Jim's?**

  If you have time, go around the circle and give everyone an opportunity to answer the question. Be sure they understand that "I'm not sure" is a perfectly appropriate response. It can take a lifetime to develop a response to suffering and loss. And Christians differ, as we've just seen.

  Is there another perspective on this issue that you could share with your group? Yes. It's in between the two extremes depicted in the case studies. This middle position holds that God does not *cause* accidents and suffering and loss, even for the best of reasons. But God does *allow* such things to happen—for reasons often apparent only to God, who can turn evil into good.

5 CLOSING
5 minutes

Summarize the session by saying something along these lines:

To say that God isn't present in our suffering is to ignore how Jesus Christ participated in the pain of the world through his death on the cross. Jesus conquered death and promised to prepare a place for us (John 14:1-6). As Paul promised in Romans 8, nothing can separate us from the love of God through Christ Jesus our Lord. To ask "Why?" is a natural reaction for humans who like to understand and be in control of their lives. To respond in faith when life seems unfair is, in effect, a way to stay close to the God who gets us out of nothing, but through everything! So it's not really a question of God's fairness but our faithfulness.

Close the session by asking the group to stand in a circle. Ask each person to repeat this promise from God to the person on his or her right: **God says, "[name], never will I leave you; never will I forsake you" (Heb. 13:5).**

OPTIONS

OPTIONAL INTERVIEW

Handout 5 ("Optional Interview") extends today's session into the coming week by inviting group members to talk to a person who has suffered from an illness or tragic event. Read the directions from the handout:

People who have gone through a painful experience are often the best teachers on the subject. Maybe you know someone who has experienced a loss or who is struggling through a serious illness. If so, contact the person and ask if he or she would be willing to talk about the experience with you. Try to set up a time to meet face to face. If that's not possible, ask if you may conduct the interview over the phone.

You'll want to point out that doing the interview is a great way to help our own faith grow. Remind your teens to ask permission to share the information with the group at the next meeting. They should respect the wishes of the person regarding the use of their story.

OPTIONAL BIBLE STUDY: WHO'S TO BLAME?
15 minutes

If you're doing this course during a retreat and have some extra time, you may want to add this Bible study to those in step 3 of the regular session (you could assign it to a third small group or use it with the entire class). The study is on Handout 6 ("Optional Bible Study: Who's to Blame?").

1. What one word or phrase stands out to you in the passage? Don't allow time for kids to explain the reason that they picked the word or phrase. Just name it for now.

2. Why do you think the disciples asked the question, "Rabbi, who sinned: this man or his parents?" We often feel more in control of a situation if we can understand it in terms of a cause-and-effect relationship. We want to make order out of mystery, so we try to pin the blame on someone or something.

3. Does our own wrongdoing ever cause an illness or other problem? Explain. In some instances, of course, people are clearly to blame for their own troubles: a heavy smoker ends up with lung cancer, a heavy drinker with a diseased liver; a spendthrift ends up bankrupt; a rude person ends up being shunned. And so on.

4. Give some examples of how we might make a false connection between our (bad) behavior and our illness or other difficulty. Teens sometimes do wrongfully blame themselves when bad things happen. For example, someone might think her bad attitude toward her parents caused their divorce. Someone else might connect his cheating at school and his coming down with a world-class case of the flu. Kids need to hear they shouldn't make these quick and easy, cause-and-effect connections—not with themselves, not with others.

5. What can you learn from this story about Christ's response to suffering in the world? What is the message for us today in this story? Jesus teaches us that the disciples were asking the wrong question. They were looking for blame. In part, the message for us today is that God is present when we suffer, and God's desire is for us to be whole, physically and spiritually. Even as Jesus restored the sight of the blind man, so he can provide spiritual wholeness to all who confess him as Lord. In him there is hope!

Loss Through Divorce

SCRIPTURE

Genesis 2:23-24; Ecclesiastes 4:9-12; Ephesians 5:22-33; Mark 10:2-12; 1 John 4:7-12

TODAY'S THEME

I'm divorced. There, I wrote it and the secret is out. Divorce is contrary to God's desire for us. So let me be very clear: I believe that divorce is a sin and that the Bible teaches divorce is a sin. I believe that lying to your parents, stealing money from a friend, cheating on a school exam, and gossiping about members of your youth group are equally as sinful. I also believe in forgiveness and God's grace. God can make all things new.

We live in a society where nearly half of all marriages end in divorce. Here are some recent statistics about marriages that end in divorce:

- 11 percent of the adult population is currently divorced.
- 25 percent of adults have had at least one divorce during their lifetime.
- Divorce rates among conservative Christians were much higher than for other faith groups.
- 27 percent of born-again Christians have been divorced.
- 21 percent of atheists or agnostics have been divorced.

—Statistics from Barna Research Group published on www.religioustolerance.org.

As the statistics reveal, members of our churches are not exempt from the struggle of maintaining healthy marriages. Sadly, when Christian couples are struggling in their marriage, the last place they want to go for help is the church. They often hide their struggle from public view because of their fear of embarrassment or alienation. As a result, their troubled marriage is a "family secret."

In this session you should focus on how divorce is a form of loss and separation for everyone involved. Children affected by divorce are faced with a wide range of issues. They need to belong to communities of faith who unconditionally love them as they face the many changes in their life.

GOALS OF THE MEETING

- to identify some of the feelings of teens when their parents divorce
- to identify some of the losses they experience as a result of divorce
- to explore God's desire for marriage and the forgiveness available for those who fail
- to identify ways to care for those who experience divorce in their family

MATERIALS

1. Bibles
2. Handouts 7-8, pens
3. Newsprint, markers
4. Notecards

THEME THOUGHTS

If you are ministering to youth today, you are ministering to teens affected by divorce. While the church should continue to explore various means of ministry to strengthen marriages and families, we cannot ignore those who feel the pain and loss of divorce. They should not feel isolated from the church. Rather, the church should embrace them and encourage them in their faith. Their faith may be the only security they have to hold on to during turbulent times of change.

Imagine what it must be like to have your family torn apart. For some teens it means

- the loss of the home they have always lived in.
- the loss of their established social group if they have to move away.
- the loss of time with at least one of their parents.
- the loss of financial stability, which can limit their involvement in activities.

- the loss of their established church home.
- the loss of hope in having their own loving relationships.

It is important to discuss how teens experiencing divorce in their families may feel so that we can respond lovingly rather than judgmentally. Too often we ignore talking about the pain and loss of divorce in an effort to avoid embarrassing a group member whose family has experienced divorce, and so we miss the opportunity to be the hearts and hands of Christ. The message these teens may be hearing is that those folks from church really don't care about their problems.

Teenagers who experience divorce often feel the pain of emotional abandonment. As Christians, we must use every opportunity to share with them the message of God's grace, forgiveness, and hope. As teachers and leaders, we can demonstrate love to those who may feel unloved. We can help teens process any sense of guilt that they contributed to or are responsible for their parents' divorce. We can provide them an opportunity and a safe place to vent their anger, disappointment, sense of relief, or fear. Young people need to be assured that there is hope beyond their loss and pain, especially if they feel that God has been unfair to them.

MEETING PLAN

1 DIVORCE: IT HURTS!
10 minutes

Open today's meeting with a few brief comments along these lines:

Today we're going to be talking about divorce and its impact on families. I realize that for some of you whose parents have divorced, this might be like scraping old wounds. Talking about divorce can also be painful and scary for those of us whose parents are struggling in their marriage. Even if our parents get along great, talking about divorce and knowing how to relate to kids going through a divorce in their families is not easy. But we can't simply avoid this topic and hope it will go away. Because it won't. (You may want to cite some statistics here—see "Today's Theme.") **So let's be honest and sensitive and caring as we talk about this, OK?**

Divide into groups of three or four persons each. Give each group a sheet of newsprint and a marker. Ask the groups to designate someone to be the recorder. Explain that they'll have five minutes to describe the impact of divorce on kids their age. In other words, how do kids whose parents have divorced (or are divorcing) feel and think and behave? What's going through their heads? Emphasize that there are no "right" answers here. The groups should just brainstorm together and jot down words and phrases that describe feelings, thoughts, and actions.

After five minutes, have the groups post their newsprint lists on the walls. Have someone from each group quickly present their list to the class. You may want to add some of the following, if the kids don't mention them:

- guilt for somehow causing or at least contributing to the divorce
- anger at Mom or Dad or God, at life in general
- sense of abandonment, loneliness
- depressed, feeling of hopelessness
- uprooted from friends
- uprooted from relatives
- feeling that life is unfair
- let-down feeling
- can't trust anyone anymore
- want to be left alone
- not helped by church or feel judged by church
- worry about money—may need to get job to help family
- split loyalty between mom and dad—trying to please both
- embarrassed by parental dating
- non-accepting toward Mom or Dad's new love
- easily upset
- vulnerable to peer pressure
- unhappy
- want help but don't know how to ask for it

Conclude this step by asking everyone to think about the following two questions as we explore this issue some more:

- **How can someone survive the pain of their parents' divorce?**
- **What can others do to help someone whose parents are divorcing?**

Explain that you'll return to these questions later in the meeting.

2 CASE STUDY: CAUGHT IN THE MIDDLE

15 minutes

Have everyone stay in the same group as in the previous step. Distribute Handout 7 ("Case Study: Caught in the Middle"). The case study focuses on one of the stresses faced by kids whose parents have divorced: "Should I live with Mom or Dad?"

Ask the groups to read the case and then discuss the three questions that follow:

- **What reasons would John have to stay with his mom?**
- **What reasons would John have to move in with his dad?**
- **What would you advise John to do? Why?**

Give the groups no more than ten minutes. Then ask each group to report on what they would advise John to do, and why. There's no "right" answer here, of course—the object is to help the group sense just one of the frustrations and difficulties children whose parents divorce may face. It would be great if you have some differing advice from the small groups. You'll want to help the group see that it's a tough issue for the parents as well as for John.

VARIATION

Have the small groups role-play their advice to John. One person in the group can take the role of John, the other can be advisors. If the groups are large enough, other kids could play John's mom and dad.

If you don't have time for more small group activity, simply work through the case study and questions with the entire class.

3 BIBLE STUDY: WHAT GOD WANTS FOR MARRIAGE

20 minutes

Raise the question of what a loving marriage relationship looks like. In other words, What are the traits of a good marriage?

To answer that question, ask for volunteers to read the following passages aloud. After each passage is read, list (on newsprint or board) the trait or traits of a good marriage that it suggests.

- Genesis 2:23-24 (unity, oneness, loyalty to each other)
- Ecclesiastes 4:9-12 (help each other when one is in need; defend each other; be concerned about each other's needs)
- Ephesians 5:22-33 (love each other; serve each other; care for each other; respect each other—as Christ loves his church)
- 1 John 4:7-12 (love each other as God as loved us, unselfishly, completely, sacrificially)

Point to your list and comment that this is the way God intended marriage to be. Continue by asking the following questions:

- **Why do you think people get married?**
- **Why do some marriages end in divorce?**

Ask for a volunteer to read Mark 10:2-12 aloud. Continue with questions along these lines:

- **Why do you think Jesus speaks so harshly about divorce?** It goes against God's plan for a marriage (see v. 9). It breaks the covenant made before God. It hurts many people, not just those getting the divorce. Marriages are meant to be permanent; divorce is contrary to God's will.

- **Is it wrong for, say, a woman who has been abused by her husband, or a husband whose wife has been unfaithful, to get a divorce?** No. The Bible and the church allow for divorce in certain situations. "The church must apply biblical principles to concrete situations in the light of its best understanding of what happened in a particular divorce" (*Doctrinal and Ethical Positions,*

Christian Reformed Church in North America, 2000, p. 18).

- **Who is affected when parents divorce?** Among those affected are the children, the husband and wife, the families of each spouse, the friends of each spouse, the friends of their children, the church members who related to their family, coworkers, and classmates.

- **What are the losses a child of divorce experiences?** Please see the list in "Theme Thoughts." Note that losses are financial, social, emotional, spiritual, and relational—in other words, virtually every aspect of being human is affected by divorce.

- **What do you think about divorce?**

- **What must God think about divorce in our society today?**

- **What can you do to prepare for a marriage that will not end in divorce?** Keep God at the center of the relationship; take time to develop a healthy relationship (statistics show the divorce rate is higher for those who marry before age twenty-five); wait until marriage before having sex (sex before marriage not only violates God's command but also focuses the relationship on sexual need rather than on emotional commitment; seek premarital counseling.

- **What should the message of the church be to individuals and families who have experienced divorce?** "The church must minister with special concern to those involved in the traumatic experience of divorce, speaking with clarity where sinful conduct is overt and apparent. . . . The church must be a place of acceptance and support for those who have been divorced and for their children" (*Doctrinal and Ethical Positions,* Christian Reformed Church in North America, 2000, p. 18). Please see "Theme Thoughts" for further comments.

4 HOW TO SURVIVE, HOW TO HELP
10 minutes

Call on someone to come forward and sit in front of the group (or cluster the group around the person). Be careful to choose someone who has not experienced the divorce of his or her parents. Say something like this: **Imagine that [name] came home from school one day and found Mom and Dad waiting to talk to him or her. Soberly they broke the news that they were getting a divorce. What advice would you suggest that might help him or her survive the divorce?** Hand out notecards and have kids write at least one piece of advice on the cards. Collect the cards and ask the person you've chosen to read them aloud. You may want to supplement their comments with some of the following (if you use any of these, ask the kids what they think of them; don't present the ideas as the "final word").

- Avoid a guilt trip—realize that you didn't cause your parents' divorce.
- Recognize that while your parents no longer love each other, they still love you.
- Realize that your friends are going to stay your friends, no matter what.
- Talk to your pastor or to a favorite teacher, a relative, or another caring, responsible adult about your feelings.
- Stay close to God.
- Recognize that some feelings of anger and depression are normal and will pass or greatly diminish with time.
- Work on forgiving your parents.
- Stay close to friends who affirm and encourage you; avoid friends who dwell on the negatives.

Call someone else forward (again, someone whose parents haven't divorced). Say something like this: **This time I'd like you to imagine that this person is a close friend of yours whose parents have recently divorced. What could you do or say that might help your friend through this difficult situation?** Distribute another notecard to each person and ask everyone to think of at least two things they could say or do. They may think of positive things to do and negative things to avoid doing.

Again, collect the cards and have the student you've selected read them aloud. If necessary, supplement ideas from the kids with some of the following, asking the kids what they think of the suggestions:

Do:

- "Be there" for your friend when he or she needs you.
- Bring up the issue and ask directly how your friend is handling things.
- Listen sympathetically without offering quick and easy advice.
- Assure your friend of your concern.
- Pray faithfully for your friend, and let him or her know you are praying too.
- As much as possible, continue your relationship on the same basis it was before the divorce.
- Invite your friend to attend church with your family, especially if his or her parents no longer attend. Ask him or her to go to youth group with you.
- Go with your friend to games, parties, school functions, and so on.
- Introduce your friend to others who have been through a divorce.
- Help your friend see the ways God is still present in his or her life.
- Remind your friend that God cares and is there for him or her.

Don't:

- Ignore the issue, hoping it will go away.
- Take sides with your friend against one of the parents.
- Take offense if your friend has a negative attitude toward adults and authority and life in general.
- Act as if divorce is no big deal because it happens all the time.
- Gossip about your friend's situation.

You may want to offer to duplicate your list for them and distribute it at the next meeting.

VARIATION

If some kids in your group have gone through a divorce (or are going through one now), you may want to let them tell (a) how they "survived" the divorce, and (b) how they would like to be treated by their friends.

5 CLOSING: "BRANDON'S MESS" AND PRAYER

10 minutes

Distribute Handout 8 ("Brandon's Mess") and read it aloud to the group. Ask them what they think the story has to say to us when we are caught in the mess made by divorce in our families. Talk briefly about the message of forgiveness and healing that our Father in heaven offers to all who are caught in the mess of a divorce—to parents who had good intentions but messed up; to kids who are caught in the mess and may be feeling angry or alone or unloved.

Take a moment to ask if there are any additional questions about divorce that group members would like to discuss later (as part of session 4). Jot down any such questions on a sheet of newsprint.

Close with a circle prayer, inviting kids to pray aloud for parents, for kids of parents who are struggling in their marriage or who are divorcing, and kids of parents who have gone through a divorce, and for all others who feel the impact of a divorce (it's not necessary to name specific persons).

Close the prayer yourself by thanking God for unconditional love, forgiveness, and healing grace.

OPTIONS

OPTIONAL INTERVIEW FOLLOW-UP

5 minutes

If you used Handout 5 in Meeting 1 and asked kids to talk to someone who has gone through a painful experience, begin today's meeting by asking for brief reports. You may also want to share a story from your own experience. Use whatever stories are shared to introduce today's theme of divorce. It's a different type of loss in one's life.

ALTERNATE STEP 1

10-15 minutes

Rather than have small groups make lists describing the impact of divorce on teens, let them express that impact visually. Provide some or all of the following art supplies: construction paper, drawing paper, scissors, markers, Styrofoam cups, paper plates, and modeling clay. Invite kids working alone or in pairs to illustrate how a divorce in the family impacts kids. After five minutes, share the results. You may also want to mention some of the items listed in step 1 that describe the impact of divorce.

EXTRA MEETING
30 minutes or more

Invite a student or panel of students to share their own experience of divorce in their family. Provide the students with questions a week ahead of time to help them prepare. Select someone to lead the discussion that will be sensitive to the needs of the individual(s) sharing their story. Here are some questions you may want to use:

- How did you find out about your parent's decision to divorce? Was it done in a way that was helpful or hurtful?
- What were you feeling about the divorce?
- What reactions did you have toward your parents?
- What changes took place in your family?
- Did the divorce have any other effects on you? Does it still affect your life?
- What kinds of things did your friends say or do that you found helpful? Hurtful?
- What suggestions do you have for caring for a friend who is affected by divorce or for caring for ourselves through a divorce?

Be sure to allow time for group members to ask their own questions of the presenters as well.

Loss Through Death

Genesis 3:1-6; Deuteronomy 31:8; Ecclesiastes 3:1-4; Psalm 32:4; John 3:16; 11:32-37; 14:1-4; Romans 5:12; 1 Corinthians 15:55-57; Revelation 21:1-4

TODAY'S THEME

Death is one of the most-avoided words in our culture. Take a minute to look up the obituaries in your local paper. Read how many people have "died." More common are euphemisms like

- She passed away.
- He went to meet his Maker.
- The Lord took him home.
- Buddy has entered his eternal sleep.
- Mary is at her eternal resting place.
- Sue went to be with her Lord.
- Frank has crossed the river Jordan and is now singing with the angels.

We are often a bit shy about saying, flat out, "So-and-so died." As a society we strive to keep death hidden. In our world of hospitals and nursing homes, not many people witness the death of loved ones anymore. And right after death, the deceased is quickly shipped off to the funeral home to be beautified for those who will view the body in the days to come.

Of course, we all know better. The unavoidable reality is we all will die. "For dust you are and to dust you will return" says Genesis 3:19. It's true that two things in life are certain: death and taxes.

In spite of all the evidence to the contrary, many adolescents think of themselves as invincible. Their death seems light-years away—and in all likelihood, it is a long way off. However, most teens will have to face the death of a significant member of their family or a close friend before they graduate from high school. Demystifying death can give them a better understanding of the process and equip them to work through their grief when they do experience a loss.

Your kids should know that grief is a normal response to loss. It is not a sign of weakness. Furthermore, every person grieves differently. Teens who experience loss should be encouraged to embrace their grief as a way to work toward acceptance and resolution. While teens are often bombarded with images of death in the movies and on television, they seldom see a person grieve their loss. Even after a death in the family, the adults in teens' lives often want to protect them from further pain and so shield them from any expression of their grief.

Unfortunately, not wanting to talk about dying, death, and the grief process only complicates matters when a teen faces the death of a family member or friend.

GOALS OF THE MEETING

- to discuss death and dying openly
- to learn more about grief as a natural response to loss
- to examine God's perspective on death
- to identify appropriate ways to respond to those who have experienced a loss

MATERIALS

1. Bibles
2. Handouts 9-11, pens
3. Newsprint, markers
4. An obituary column from your local paper

THEME THOUGHTS

In her book *The American Way of Death,* Jessica Mitford points out that our culture is death-denying. Few adolescents are ever confronted with a dying person. Most are sheltered from adult conversations when death and dying are discussed.

Yet it's obvious that death is a natural part of the life process. Human beings are born, they live for a period of time, and then they die. There is no escaping death. And teens are ready to learn about death and dying beyond what they observe in the media.

Conversations with parents and teachers about death reduce the level of anxiety for kids who fear their own death. Teens benefit emotionally when their parents share their thoughts regarding issues related to death such as advanced life support, organ donation, burial or cremation, and the provision they have made for them in their will. They can be reassured that even in the worst-case scenario, there is a plan to be followed.

Teens also benefit spiritually by frank talk about death and dying. Their theological perspective expands as they begin to think through the promises of life after death.

Exploring the grief process will also aid young people who may have no concept of what to expect following the death of a loved one. You can help them to identify grief as a natural process in response to loss, and to realize that grieving takes time and that no two people grieve entirely in the same way. It may be a comfort for students to consider that even Jesus grieved at times of loss; for example, he openly wept at the death of his friend Lazarus (John 11:17-33). Such "grief work" is intentional; it takes effort on the part of the person who is in pain.

A side benefit of teaching students about grief is that they will better understand how they can reach out to others who are grieving. Doing so will also benefit them by transferring their energy from trying to answer the "why" question to responding to grief as a person of faith.

While it is impossible to ever be fully prepared to accept the death of a loved one, it's never too soon to become more informed about issues related to grieving, death, and dying.

MEETING PLAN

1 REALITY CHECK
10 minutes

Show the group a list of obituaries from your local paper. Read one or two aloud. You may want to share with the group how our society often finds ways to avoid direct talk about death and dying, even in the obituaries (see Today's Theme).

Then say something along these lines: **One thing is certain: unless the Lord returns while we're still alive, each one of us in this room will die. I will. You will. And while we hope and pray that our death is a very long way away, we really don't know that, of course. And so we need to talk with each other and with our families about death and dying.**

Give group members a minute or so to think of one way to die that they would most like to avoid (examples: falling off a tall building; trapped in a fire; of cancer; as a shooting victim; by drowning; and the like). Then ask them to share their idea of the worst way to die with one or two other people. After a couple of minutes, ask: **Do you think most people are afraid of dying? What makes them afraid of death?**

Ask the students to identify questions they have about death and dying and write them on a sheet of newsprint for later reference.

VARIATION

Instead of just reading an obituary or two to the group, hand out copies of obituaries from your local newspaper and ask the group to find other words for death and dying that are used in the obituaries. Bridge to the idea that we are often reluctant to talk about death and dying. Then continue with the rest of step 1.

2 THE BIBLE ON DEATH AND DYING
20 minutes

Distribute Handout 9 ("The Bible on Death and Dying). Read the directions on the handout:

Working with one or more others,

1. **Read your passage out loud.**
2. **Decide together on one key idea your assigned verses conveys about death and dying.**
3. **Find a creative way to express that idea to the rest of the group. Some possibilities:**

- **make a poster**
- **act it out or pantomime it**
- **write a slogan**
- **create a thirty-second radio or TV commercial**
- **create a "freeze frame" picture**
- **use your own idea**

You may at some point in your presentation read all or part of your passage to the group.

Divide into groups of two or three and assign one or more passages to each group, depending on how many students you have. Provide newsprint and markers, writing paper, and anything else you think the groups might need. Be available to suggest some creative ways to express the passages for groups that may be struggling. In general, encourage kids to take an approach that interests them and that they feel comfortable doing.

Allow ten minutes for working, then another ten for the small group presentations. Here are some key ideas about death and dying that the passages express (allow for variations!). Ask kids to write the key ideas in the space provided on the handout.

Group 1: Genesis 3:1-6; Romans 5:12
Death entered the world through the sin of Adam and Eve; since then, all people must die. You may want to expand on this a bit and talk about how fear of death is a perfectly understandable reaction, since death is evil, a result of sin. It is definitely not what God wanted for people!

Group 2: Ecclesiastes 3:1-4; John 11:32-37
In Jesus' grief over Lazarus' death, we see that grieving is an important and necessary response to death and dying. Even the Lord of life wept! Affirm the importance of expressing our grief, of sharing our fears and heartbreak with others.

Group 3: John 3:16; John 14:1-4; 1 Corinthians 15:55-57
In Jesus, we can win over death and live eternally with God. We have hope! Jesus is going to prepare a place for us. He will come back and take us to be with him forever.

Group 4: Read Deuteronomy 31:8; Psalm 23:4
When we walk through the valley of the shadow of death, we will not be alone. God is with us always. We do not need to live in fear.

You may want to summarize the Bible study by reading Revelation 21:1-4 to the class—a brief but wonderful description of what awaits us after death.

VARIATION
If you are short on time, ask each group to simply read one passage and write out its key idea. Review the findings with the entire class.

---

3 UNDERSTANDING HEALTHY GRIEF
10-15 minutes

Distribute Handout 10 ("Myths of Grief Inventory"). Ask students to complete the form, then walk through the statement with them and indicate what the authors of the statement consider the best response (the survey and many of the comments below are adapted from materials presented in a workshop by Dr. Susan J. Zonnebelt-Smeenge and Dr. Robert C. DeVries. Used by permission).

1. When someone you love has died, time will eventually allow you to get over your grief.

False. Time is necessary to the healing process but is only one aspect of effective grieving. In addition to taking time, grief requires intentional "work" (see end of this step for details)

2. Having someone you care about die suddenly (as in a car accident) is far harder to deal with than having a loved one die as a result of a long-term illness.

False. While sudden deaths stun and shock us, watching a loved one suffer is one of the hardest things for humans to endure. Both sudden deaths and slow deaths of those we love take a huge physical, emotional, and spiritual toll. Being able to anticipate grief (knowing that your loved one is going to die) does not make the grieving process any easier, although it may decrease the shock or numbness following the death.

3. After the death of someone you love, you should try not to think too much about the loss. In that way the painful feelings can slowly ease away.

False. We can't deal with our grief by pretending it isn't there. If we suppress our painful thoughts now, they may well emerge later and be far more difficult to deal with then.

4. You should think only about the positive side of your relationship with your deceased loved one; since he or she is no longer here, it would be disloyal to recall the negative aspects of your relationship.

False. Blocking out unpleasant memories is not an emotionally healthy thing to do. DeVries and Zonnebelt-Smeenge insist on experiencing *all* of the emotions associated with the death of our loved one.

5. You will eventually begin to feel better if you try to appear to be happy (even if you feel awful) and accept social invitations (even if you don't feel like it).

False. If you feel awful or do not want to accept social invitations but you go anyway, this will add to your emotional stress rather than reduce it. Perhaps you need to take a "rain check," knowing that you will eventually be able to be involved again. The healthy way to behave is to be guided by the way we think and the way we feel about certain things. Zonnebelt-Smeenge and DeVries refer to this as "congruence."

6. You can resolve old remaining conflicts that existed with the person who died, even though you can no longer talk together.

True. Carrying old grudges or hurts beyond the grave isn't a healthy or Christian thing to do. Even though a person has died, you can resolve old conflicts through writing letters to the deceased person (though, of course, they can't actually read them), acknowledging how you may have contributed to the conflict, and learning that forgiveness basically comes from within yourself through Christ. We can forgive others even when we no longer have a relationship with them. Forgiveness does not mean that we no longer see what the person did as wrong. It means that we will no longer hold a grudge that creates a bitter spirit.

7. Having fun or laughing while in the grieving process may indicate that you really no longer feel hurt or miss the person who died.

False. Grieving people often feel guilty about this. We shouldn't. Better to view the lighter moments during the grieving process as gifts of God's healing grace, part of the restoration process.

8. Men should try to keep their emotions in check and really should not weep in public or otherwise openly show their grief over the death of someone they love.

False. This myth represents a long-standing notion that while it's OK for females to openly express their emotions, real men ought to go by their heads more than their hearts and exhibit self-control and strength, especially during times of tragedy and death. Please lay this myth to rest and affirm that grief is a normal response to any loss, regardless of whether one is male or female. Jesus himself openly wept over the death of Lazarus.

9. After you've lost someone you love, your happiness will never be as complete as it was before—but you do have wonderful memories to provide comfort.

False. DeVries and Zonnebelt-Smeenge point out that while resolving our grief means *never* forgetting the loved one, and while memories are precious possessions, they ought not to control our emotions on a daily basis. We are free to live life again fully in the present and remember the deceased when we choose to do so. By God's grace, we can again be happy and fulfilled people who are independent of the relationship we had with the deceased.

10. If you had a happy and fulfilling life prior to the loss of your loved one, you will likely be happy again in the next phase of your life.

True. We need to reinvest in life without the presence of the person we loved. A person mourning the death of a loved one has experienced deep grief, but eventually, say the authors of the survey, this can be seen as an opportunity to begin again in a new and fresh way.

Conclude this step by giving kids a summary of what it means to grieve in a healthy and Christian way. You may want them to take notes on the back of Handout

10. Use your own ideas and whatever you wish of the following (again, we are indebted to the survey authors for many of these thoughts).

- Remember God's promise in Deuteronomy 31:6: "The LORD your God goes with you; he will never leave you nor forsake you." It's comforting to know that God stays at our side, even when we may not feel like staying in touch with God.
- Accept the reality of death. The person you love has died and is unable to return.
- Let your emotions show. Don't try to hide how you feel. Showing and sharing your emotions can help in the healing process.
- Honor the memory of your loved one, but don't live in the past. Establishing traditions or rituals to honor your loved one may be helpful and healing; for example, placing flowers in the sanctuary on the day they died (or on their birthday or anniversary or other special day).
- Rediscover who you are as an individual, apart from the person who died. Begin again in a new and fresh way.

4 HELPING OTHERS AND CLOSING PRAYER
10 minutes

Ask the group to think about how they would like to be treated if they had recently experienced the death of a parent or grandparent, brother or sister, other relative, or very close friend. Allow a minute or so to think, then go around the circle and ask each person to complete the following statement: **If this happened to me, I would like it if my friends would (or would not) . . .** Let kids know it's OK to repeat ideas if they can't think of something new to add.

You may want to supplement their list with some of the following, if they weren't mentioned:

- be there for me and listen—or sit in silence with me
- pray for me and my family
- talk to me about my feelings
- be sad with me
- give me a hug
- understand if I say and do things that aren't like the usual me

- not say well-meant but unhelpful things, like "It's for the best," or "God wanted this to happen," or "a year from now things will be better."
- not pretend everything's the same as before
- caringly challenge me to move on with my life if I seem to be stuck

Look at the newsprint sheet on which you've listed questions about death from the group. As time permits, discuss questions that haven't been answered in this session (or hold them until the final session next week).

Close by giving everyone an opportunity to pray for persons who have experienced a death in their family or the death of a friend. End the prayer yourself by thanking Jesus for giving us victory over death.

Distribute Handout 11 ("A Guide for Difficult Conversations about Death and Dying") before everyone leaves. Encourage kids to use at least some of this guide with their parents this week, if possible. We'll discuss their reactions/responses at the beginning of our next meeting.

OPTIONS

ALTERNATIVE CLOSING PRAYER
As a substitute for the prayer described in step 4, have kids write a personal prayer to God expressing their feelings about death and dying (their own or others). Topics could include fear of death, doubt or concern about salvation, thanks for victory over death, and so on. Prayers can be read silently to close your session.

FIELD TRIP
Plan a visit to a funeral home and have the director give a presentation on how families plan for a funeral. What choices must be made? How expensive is a funeral? What are options available? What are the personal benefits one might expect from having visitation before the funeral?

Loss Through Tragedy

SCRIPTURE

Proverbs 15:22; Ecclesiastes 4:9-10, 12; Deuteronomy 31:8; John 9:1-3; 2 Corinthians 1:3-11

TODAY'S THEME

Our meeting today focuses on loss through the unexpected tragedies that life sometimes throws at us. Sometimes we ourselves experience the loss; other times we are called to respond to others who experience the loss. Of course, nothing can fully prepare us to "be ready" for loss in our lives. However, anticipating loss as a part of life can help us know how to live in response to a loss and how to be present to others when they experience a loss.

Remind your group that Christians have hope in a God "who gets us out of nothing and through everything." A contemporary theologian, Jurgen Moltman, was asked, "Why does God allow suffering?" He responded, "The better question would be, Why does God suffer suffering?" The rephrased question more closely identifies where God is in the mixture and complexity of unexplainable events. Do we really believe that God is present in the midst of the pain and suffering of a broken world?

Adopting this way of thinking may be the only way to face the reality of catastrophic events that claim the lives of innocent people: school shootings, earthquakes, famine, drought, floods, destructive storms, a drunk driver who kills three generations of family members and his pregnant wife, a father who takes his own life, a terrorist attack. Knowing that God is present in such tragedies and is not absent from the pain does not provide an answer, but it does provide hope.

As you examine this final section, continue to give group members the opportunity to ask questions without yielding to the need to give simplistic answers.

GOALS OF THE MEETING

- to discuss perceptions of tragic loss
- to react and respond to a story of tragic loss
- to explore how we can find hope and help in God and others
- to emphasize the importance of the ministry of presence

MATERIALS

1. Bibles
2. Handouts 12-13, pens
3. Newsprint, markers
4. Accounts of tragic events from newspapers and magazines

THEME THOUGHTS

It's impossible for the kids you teach to escape hearing about tragedies that happen every day. If they don't hear about it on the radio or TV, they'll catch it on the Internet or in the local paper.

Our lives are full of stories about tragic losses. Consider the following statistics:

- Some 28 separate school shootings have been recorded since February 1996, resulting in 15 deaths and 10 serious injuries (www.keystosaferschools.com).
- Suicide ranks third as a cause of death among young (age 15-24) Americans, behind accidents and homicide (www.crisishotline.org/strategies/term.htm).
- On average, every two hours and five minutes, one young person kills him- or herself (www.iusb.edu/~jmcintos/1997data.pdf).
- On average, every year in the United States, 146 people die in floods, 90 people die who are hit by lightening, 69 people die in tornadoes, and 17 people die in hurricanes (www.crh.noaa.gov/lmk/tornado1/fslide25.htm).

- Presently 25,000 people are killed each year in alcohol-related accidents. Youth are responsible for 42 percent of these deaths (www.nh-dwi.com/caip-206.htm).

At some time, most of the kids in your group will have to deal with a family member's suicide, a friend's death in an automobile accident, or some other form of tragic loss. Perhaps even today your congregation prayed for an individual or family hit by a tragedy of one kind or another. After all, the church is supposed to be a refuge for survivors, a place of healing for the broken, a source of hope for the questioner, right? So what happens when there are no clear answers to our questions?

Some of the tragic events in life are easily explained by circumstances. Others are more puzzling, and the "why" question comes popping back. In today's meeting, you'll want to help kids realize that we live in an imperfect world that is tremendously complex. Paint a picture of a God who "suffers suffering," and is present in our own suffering and loss. Focus on allowing kids to express their feelings and ask their questions.

As you explore today's topic, be sensitive to students who have faced their own tragic loss experience. Model through your example a person willing to practice a "ministry of presence." Following are some guidelines for simply "being present" in the wake of a crisis.

- Offer your time. Spending time with kids shows them—better than any words you might say—that you care about what's going on in their lives. However, also respect their decision to not choose you as the adult they turn to.
- When a teen is ready to share, simply sit back and be quiet. Avoid offering clichéd advice and jumping to your own conclusions.
- Validate their feelings. Let kids know that what they're feeling is normal and OK. Don't minimize their feelings or the impact of an event in their lives.
- Allow kids to be angry at God and to voice their disappointments or frustrations with God.
- Have fun. Sometimes kids need a reminder that they're allowed to still just be kids.

- Once a teen has come to you, ask if you may pray for him or her. If you tell someone that you'll pray for them, make sure you follow through.
- Don't get in over your head. While most often teens need friends rather than psychologists, rely on your instincts if you feel that a kid needs more than you can give. If you need to involve someone with more expertise, contact your pastor for a referral.

---

1 REVIEW OF "DIFFICULT CONVERSATIONS" (OPTIONAL)
5 minutes

If you encouraged kids to discuss Handout 11 ("A Guide for Difficult Conversations about Dying and Death") with their parents, ask them if they had a chance to do so. Ask how parents reacted to the questions and if the discussion helped in any way. Even if only one or two kids have something to share, their comments might encourage others to talk to their parents about dying and death.

Summarize by saying something like this: **Death is a part of life. We all will die. As Christians we are not exempt from the grief that accompanies a death of a family member or friend. However, we can work through our grief with the assurance of God's promise for life. Grief work is intentional. It takes time. We need to be willing to embrace others who are grieving. Today as we wrap up this series of meetings, we'll look at another kind of loss.**

---

2 IN THE NEWS
10 minutes

Write the following on newsprint:

- Kurt Cobaine
- Santee, California
- TWA Flight 800
- Littleton, Colorado
- Taber, Alberta
- Nicole Simpson
- Ethnic Albanians, Kosovo
- Princess Diana
- Murrah Federal Building, Oklahoma City

- Tropical Storm Allison
- World Trade Center

Ask students if they can identify any common links with the words you've listed. They should recognize that the names and places are linked by a tragic and sudden loss of life.

Take a moment to identify the list of tragedies with the group:

- Kurt Cobaine: suicide, lead singer of Nirvana, died April 8, 1994
- Santee, California: site of school shooting killing 2 students, May 2001
- TWA Flight 800: 230 people killed when their plane exploded
- Littleton, Colorado: site of school shooting killing 15 students, April 1999
- Taber, Alberta: site of "copycat" school shooting, April 1999
- Nicole Simpson: former wife of O.J. Simpson, murdered June 1994
- Ethnic Albanians, Kosovo: "ethnic cleansing"— mass murder of thousands of innocent people
- Princess Diana: killed in an automobile accident, August 1997
- Murrah Federal Building, Oklahoma City: site of the single most devastating act of terrorism in the United States, a bombing that killing 168 people, April 1995
- Tropical Storm Allison: killed 43 persons in U.S., June 2001
- World Trade Center: destroyed by a terrorist attack on September 11, 2001, killing almost 3,000 people

Follow-up with questions like these:

- **What are some other, more recent examples of sudden and tragic deaths?**
- **What do you think about when you hear about such tragedies?**
- **Have you ever been faced by a tragic loss in your life?**
- **Have you ever had to comfort someone who suffered a tragic and sudden loss?**

3 CASE STUDY: DEALING WITH TRAGEDY
10-15 minutes

Distribute Handout 12 ("Case Study: Dealing with Tragedy") and ask for a volunteer to read it aloud. Use questions like these to discuss the case:

- **If you were in Edie's situation, what would you be feeling? What questions would you have?**
- **What were Edie's feelings about her dad's suicide? What questions did she have?**
- **How did Edie get through the tragedy of her father's suicide?**
- **Based on Edie's insights and your own ideas, how might you help someone who has experienced a tragedy in his or her life?** (The issue of helping others will be discussed again later in the session; you needn't cover all the bases here.)

4 BIBLE STUDY: HOPE HELP, AND HEALING
25-30 minutes

For your Bible study today, have kids get into groups of three to six persons each. If you have fewer than six students, have everyone stay in a single group. Explain that you'd like the small groups to work through today's Bible study on their own, without your supervision and without reporting back to the entire class. Distribute Handout 13 ("Bible Study: Hope, Help, and Healing") and read the directions to the class:

As you work your way through this handout with your small group, please have different group members read the comments aloud to the group. Stop when you come to one of the following symbols and follow the directions:

 Talk over with your group.

 Go around the circle and have everyone respond.

 Jot down your personal, private response.

It's possible, even probable, that you will not graduate from high school without facing a sudden crisis or tragedy: an accident seriously injures a family member; a classmate is shot while working at a local convenience store; a good friend drowns in a boating accident; a tornado causes enormous damage and loss of life in your town. If you are fortunate enough not to have encountered a tragedy like this, you may well have a close friend who will need your help. While we can never be "ready" for such unwelcome events in our lives, it does help to equip ourselves with a basic understanding of the hope, help, and healing promised by God in the Bible.

Provide Bibles for every group member. Give groups twenty minutes to work their way through the handout. Make yourself available to the groups should they need an explanation of a question or other help.

After twenty minutes (or when most groups are finished), take a moment to ask the following questions:

- **What, if anything, did you find most helpful about this Bible study?**
- **Are there any questions you'd like to talk about with the whole class?**

You may want to spend a little time talking about the very last question on the handout: **How can we be present in the life of those who suffer tragic losses?**

Your kids could benefit from a variety of ideas on this question. You may want to record their responses on a sheet of newsprint and give kids paper on which to copy your list. Here are some ideas (some may be repeats from last week's session about loss through death):

- spend time with them, either in person or on the phone
- ask them for the privilege of praying for them
- be a good listener
- be specific when offering help (not, "Let me know if there's anything I can do to help," but, "Would you like some help catching up on that science project tomorrow after school?")

- help get them re-involved in youth group and social stuff at school by offering them a ride, sitting with them, and so on
- be sympathetic but avoid any impression of pity
- drop whatever else you're doing when they want to talk
- encourage them spiritually if they're having doubts about God and their faith
- remind them, when appropriate, that God loves them and is hurting with them
- avoid quick and easy answers for getting over their loss

You may want to conclude this part of the session with this comment: **One writer** (Robert Veninga, in his book *A Gift of Hope: How We Survive Our Tragedies*), **suggests that "almost without exception, those who survive tragedy give credit to one person who stood by them, supported them, and gave them a sense of hope."** Encourage kids to be that person, when and if God places them in the position of comforting a friend who has suffered a loss.

VARIATION

If you choose the option for step 2 instead of the case study, you could bring in the case study at the end of step 3 as a source of ideas for helping others.

4 CLOSING
10 minutes

Post the list(s) of questions the group members raised in meeting 1 and throughout the course. Ask if these questions have been adequately covered and take time to address any that the group would like to discuss further. Invite any additional questions that have surfaced over the past several weeks.

Close by having kids pray for concerns raised by others in the group, especially concerns that are related to the losses we talked about in this course. Here's a method that works well with teens:

- Give notecards to two students and ask them to jot down (neatly) concerns, requests, thanks, or items of praise from the group.
- Invite group members to state their concerns, requests, and so on, aloud.
- Have the note-takers distribute their cards to the group at random (if anyone gets his or her own card, he or she should exchange it for another).
- Have group members read their card aloud for the closing prayer.

Reading a prayer makes praying aloud easier for shy kids—and it enables kids to pray for concerns raised by others.

After the prayer, encourage everyone to keep asking questions and to remember that when life seems unfair, it's never about God's fairness, but our faithfulness in continuing to seek God. God is able to handle our anger, frustration, doubt, sadness, and questions.

You may also want to distribute Handout 14 ("Evaluation Form") and ask everyone to complete it. There's also an evaluation form for you to fill out at the back of this book. We appreciate your effort in completing it so that we can better serve your needs in the future.

OPTIONS

WHAT WOULD YOU DO?

This is a substitute for the case study in step 2. Begin by dividing into groups of two to four persons each. Give each group a recent newspaper or magazine article that tells the story of some sort of tragedy. Ask the group members to

- Read key parts of the article to the members of their group.
- Share an initial response of how you think the families of the victims feel.
- Write down questions you think the victim's families might be asking.
- Discuss how they might respond to someone who approached them who was affected by the tragedy.

You may want to write out these directions on newsprint or a chalkboard. Allow ten minutes for groups to work and five minutes for reporting. Keep reports brief, asking each group to summarize their article and share their answers to the questions above.

After the reports, proceed with the Bible Study in step 3. If you wish, you could still use Handout 12 at the end of step 3 as a source of ideas on how to help people who are going through a tragic loss.

GUEST PRESENTER

Perhaps you know of someone in your congregation or community who suffered a major tragedy, struggled to make sense of it, and came out with a stronger faith than before. If such a person is willing and able to talk about his or her experiences, your group might benefit from a brief presentation and discussion time.

Where Is God?

The following is an excerpt from Elie Wiesel's book *Night,* which describes his own experience in a concentration camp. Wiesel was fifteen years old at the time he witnessed this tragedy. Here he describes the execution of a young boy who worked as a servant for a Dutchman who was smuggling arms. The boy was sentenced to death by the SS for failing to cooperate.

One day when we came back from work, we saw three gallows rearing up in the assembly place, three black crows. Roll call, SS all around us, machine guns trained: the traditional ceremony. Three victims in chains—and one of them the little servant, the sad-eyed angel.

The SS seemed more preoccupied, more disturbed than usual. To hang a young boy in front of thousands of spectators was no light matter.

The head of the camp read the verdict. All eyes were on the child. He was lividly pale, almost calm, biting his lips. The gallows threw its shadow over him.

This time the Lagerkapo refused to act as executioner. Three SS replaced him.

The three victims mounted together onto chairs.

The three necks were placed at the same moment within the nooses.

"Long live liberty!" cried the two adults.

But the child was silent.

"Where is God? Where is He?" someone behind me asked.

At a sign from the head of the camp, the three chairs tipped over.

Total silence throughout the camp. On the horizon the sun was setting.

"Bare your heads!" yelled the head of the camp. His voice was raucous. We were weeping.

"Cover your heads!"

Then the march past began. The two adults were no longer alive. Their tongues hung swollen, blue-tinged. But the third rope was still moving; being so light, the child was still alive. . . .

For more than half an hour he stayed there, struggling between life and death, dying in slow agony under our eyes. And we had to look him full in the face. He was still alive when I passed in front of him. His tongue was still red, his eyes not yet glazed.

Behind me, I heard the same man asking: "Where is God now?"

And I heard a voice within me answer him, "Where is He? Here He is—He is hanging here on this gallows. . . ."

That night the soup tasted of corpses.

—Excerpt from *Night* by Elie Wiesel, trans. Stella Rodway. Copyright ©1960 by MacGibbon & Kee. Copyright renewed ©1988 by The Collins Publishing Group. Reprinted by permission of Hill and Wang, A division of Farrar, Straus and Giroux, LLC.

This was the moment in Elie Wiesel's life that he lost his faith in God. Having endured already so much in the concentration camp at Buna, he could no longer believe in a God who would allow such suffering to continue to exist.

1. How do you react to this true story? What questions does it raise in your mind?

2. "Where is God?" asks one of the prisoners. What response comes to your mind in answer to this question as you read this account?

3. Sometimes bad things happen to good people. Many times people affected by a tragic event find themselves asking the "why" question. Can you think of events in your own life, from others' lives, or from news stories, that have made you want to ask God the "why" question?

4. What are some of the conclusions you or others have come to in answer to the "why" question?

5. Why do you think people often want to know answers to the "why" question?

Is **GOD** Fair?

We believe that God is all-loving, all-powerful, and all-present, yet the fact remains that there is much suffering in the world. Read each of the following statements and circle the response that best expresses your view. Do not take a lot of time on each statement.

1. God causes bad things to happen in our lives to teach us something or to accomplish a greater good in the world.

   totally agree   somewhat agree   neutral   somewhat disagree   totally disagree

2. God allows bad things to happen in our lives to teach us something or to accomplish a greater good in the world.

   totally agree   somewhat agree   neutral   somewhat disagree   totally disagree

3. God punishes people by causing bad things to happen in their lives.

   totally agree   somewhat agree   neutral   somewhat disagree   totally disagree

4. God created the world good, but as a result of sin there is suffering in the world.

   totally agree   somewhat agree   neutral   somewhat disagree   totally disagree

5. God always treats Christian people fairly.

   totally agree   somewhat agree   neutral   somewhat disagree   totally disagree

6. God treats all people fairly.

   totally agree   somewhat agree   neutral   somewhat disagree   totally disagree

7. People suffer in the world as a result of their sin.

   totally agree   somewhat agree   neutral   somewhat disagree   totally disagree

8. Accidents happen not as a result of God's choosing but as a result of peoples' bad choices.

   totally agree   somewhat agree   neutral   somewhat disagree   totally disagree

9. Accidents just happen. That is why they are called accidents.

   totally agree   somewhat agree   neutral   somewhat disagree   totally disagree

Two Great Sufferers: Job and Jesus

JOB

Job is a good man and knows it, as does everybody else including God. Then one day his cattle are stolen, his servants killed, and the wind blows down the house where his children happen to be whooping it up at the time, and not one of them lives to tell what it was they thought they had to whoop it up about. But being a good man he says only, "The Lord gave, and the Lord hath taken away. Blessed be the name of the Lord." Even when he comes down with a bad case of boils and his wife advises him to curse God and die, he manages to bite his tongue and say nothing. It's his friends who finally break the camel's back. They come to offer their condolences and hang around a full week. When Job finds them still there at the start of the second week, he curses the day he was born. He never quite takes his wife's advice and curses God, but he comes very close to it. He asks some unpleasant questions:

If God is all he's cracked up to be, how come houses blow down on innocent people? Why does a good man die of cancer in his prime while old men who can't remember their names or hold their water go on in nursing homes forever? Why are there so many crooks riding around in Cadillacs and so many children going to bed hungry at night? Job's friends offer an assortment of theological explanations, but God doesn't offer one.

God doesn't explain. He explodes. He asks Job who he thinks he is anyway. He says that to try to explain the kind of things Job wants explained would be like trying to explain

Einstein to a little-neck clam. He also, incidentally, gets off some of the greatest poetry in the Old Testament. "Hast thou entered into the treasures of the snow? Canst thou bind the sweet influences of the Pleiades? Hast thou given the horse strength and clothed his neck with thunder?"

Maybe the reason God doesn't explain to Job why terrible things happen is that he knows what Job needs isn't an explanation. Suppose that God did explain. Suppose that God were to say to Job that the reason the cattle were stolen, the crops ruined, and the children killed was thus and so, spelling everything out right down to and including the case of boils. Job would have his explanation.

And then what?

Understanding in terms of the divine economy why his children had to die, Job would still have to face their empty chairs at breakfast every morning. Carrying in his pocket straight from the horse's mouth a straight theological justification of his boils, he would still have to scratch and burn.

God doesn't reveal his grand design. He reveals himself. He doesn't show why things are as they are. He shows his face. . . .

—Frederick Buechner, *Wishful Thinking: A Theological ABC*, pp. 46-47. Copyright ©1973 by Frederick Buechner. Reprinted by permission of HarperCollins Publishers, Inc.

1. What terrible things happened to Job?

2. How did Job react?

3. How did God react? Why didn't God explain why Job suffered?

4. "God shows his face." What does this mean for us when we suffer?

5. What additional questions or comments do you have about Job and his suffering?

JESUS

They came to an area called Gethsemane. Jesus told his disciples, "Sit here while I pray." He took Peter, James, and John with him. He plunged into a sinkhole of dreadful agony. He told them, "I feel bad enough right now to die. Stay here and keep vigil with me."

Going a little ahead, he fell to the ground and prayed for a way out: "Papa, Father, you can—can't you?—get me out of this. Take this cup from me. But please, not what I want—what do you want?". . .

The soldiers brought Jesus to Golgotha, meaning "Skull Hill." They offered him a mild painkiller (wine mixed with myrrh), but he wouldn't take it. And they nailed him to the cross. They divided up his clothes and threw dice to see who would get them.

They nailed him up at nine o'clock in the morning. The charge against him—THE KING OF THE JEWS—was printed on a poster. Along with him, they crucified two criminals, one to his right, the other to his left. People passing along the road jeered, shaking their heads in mock lament: "You bragged that you could tear down the Temple and then rebuild it in three days—so show us your stuff! Save yourself! If you're really God's Son, come down from that cross!"

The high priests, along with the religion scholars, were right there mixing it up with the rest of them, having a great time poking fun at him: "He saved others—but he can't save himself! Messiah, is he? King of Israel? Then let him climb down from that cross. We'll all become believers then!" Even the men crucified alongside him joined in the mockery.

At noon the sky became extremely dark. The darkness lasted three hours. At three o'clock, Jesus groaned out of the depths, crying loudly, "Eloi, Eloi, lama sabachthani?" which means, "My God, my God, why have you abandoned me?"

Some of the bystanders who heard him said, "Listen, he's calling for Elijah." Someone ran off, soaked a sponge in sour wine, put it on a stick, and gave it to him to drink, saying, "Let's see if Elijah comes to take him down."

But Jesus, with a loud cry, gave his last breath. At that moment the Temple curtain ripped right down the middle. When the Roman captain standing guard in front of him saw that he had quit breathing, he said, "This has to be the Son of God!"

—Mark 14:32-36; 15:22-39 *(The Message)*

1. When we suffer, how might it help us to know that Jesus himself suffered?

2. God sent his own Son to suffer and die for us. What does that say about how God feels about *our* suffering?

3. What additional questions or comments do you have about Jesus and his suffering?

Case Studies:
Two Christians Respond to Life Losses

BRIAN STERNBERG

As a freshman at the University of Washington, Brian Sternberg was making sports headlines weekly. He was a gifted athlete. He set national records in pole vaulting and captured the NCAA and AAU titles in his event. On July 2, 1963, while warming up for a practice as he prepared to tour with the U.S. Track Team, Brian's life changed. Here's how he remembers the event:

If there's ever a frightening moment in trampolining, it is just as you leave the trampoline bed, on your way up. At that moment, even the most experienced gymnast sometimes gets a sensation of panic, for no good reason, that does not disappear until he is down safe on the bed again. It hit me as I took off. I got lost in midair and thought I was going to land on my hands and feet, as I had done several times before when the panic came. Instead I landed on my head.

I heard a crack in my neck, then everything was gone. My arms and legs were bouncing around in front of my eyes, but I could not feel them moving. Even before the bouncing stopped, I was yelling, "I'm paralyzed," in as loud a voice as I could, which was pretty weak because I had practically no lung power. The paralysis was affecting my breathing.

—Philip Yancey, *Where Is God When It Hurts?*
pp. 116-117

Brian survived the accident and lives today in Seattle with his mother, Helen. He has undergone several operations throughout the years, but has never regained the function of his arms or legs. He does have some use of the muscles in his shoulders. There have been numerous healing services, over five thousand cards, and prayers offered on his behalf from various places around the world. Brian's faith has remained strong, but not without challenges.

Neither Brian nor his family has ever believed this tragedy to be part of a divine plan for his life. I asked Brian how he would respond to someone who would say, "I think God caused your accident or allowed this to happen to you as part of a divine plan for your life."

"I'd tell him, 'No way!'" Brian said. "I could not love a God who would do something like this for any reason. This was an accident." His mother agreed: "We live in a world where accidents happen. There are natural laws that govern certain things like gravity. God didn't cause Brian's accident. God is love. In an effort to comfort Brian and our family, different people have suggested that this happened so that Brian could have a bigger ministry. I don't believe that. Those kind of Christian platitudes are not helpful."

While grateful for the opportunities he has had to share his faith story, Brian views it as a response to his suffering, not the reason for it. Instead of asking the "why" question,

Brian has directed his life and energy toward answering "How do I respond in faith to what has happened?" "Do your best with whatever you have," says Brian, "and don't ever limit the possibilities of how God can use you."

JIM BOWERS

On April 20, 2001, a Peruvian military jet shot down a small plane carrying missionaries Jim and Roni Bowers, their two children, and a pilot, who was flying back to their home village in Peru, South America. Their plane had mistakenly been identified as a drug-smuggling plane. Roni and her infant daughter, Charity, died in the attack. Jim and his son Cory escaped with minor injuries, and the pilot survived despite being hit in the leg by a bullet.

In the funeral service that followed a week later, Jim Bowers said he believed that God guided the bullet that killed his wife as part of a larger plan to "wake up sleeping Christians" and to arouse those who don't believe in God. "Roni and Charity were killed by the same bullet. Would you say that was a stray bullet? . . . That was a sovereign bullet."

Jim went on to say: "Could this really be God's plan for Roni and Charity? God's plan for Cory and our family? I'd like to tell you why I believe so, why I'm coming to believe so. I didn't believe that at all during the incident or tragedy, but a day or two after that, I began to see God's hand at work. . . . The one thing that convinces me God did this to Roni and Charity is the profound effect this event is having on people around the world— the interest in missionary work now. I'm hoping it will result in an increase in missionaries in the future. I'm sure it will."

—*Grand Rapids Press,* April 28, 2001

- What different responses to loss and suffering do Brian and Jim have?

- Is your own response to loss and suffering closer to Brian's or to Jim's?

Optional Interview

People who have gone through a painful experience are often the best teachers on the subject. Maybe you know someone who has experienced a loss or who is struggling through a serious illness. If so, contact the person and ask if he or she would be willing to talk about the experience with you. Try to set up a time to meet face to face. If that's not possible, ask if you may conduct the interview over the phone.

• Please describe your initial response to your illness or loss.

• Has your response changed in any way?

• Where is God in all of this for you?

• How has your outlook on life and on faith been changed or challenged as a result of your situation?

• What helpful words have people said to you? What hurtful words?

• Do you ever feel like life has been unfair to you?

• What else could I learn from you about facing difficult circumstances in my life?

• May I share your story with other members of my class?

Note: Be sure to respect the person's wishes regarding sharing the information with others. Maintain confidentiality.

Optional Bible Study:

Who's to Blame?

Walking down the street, Jesus saw a blind man from birth. His disciples asked, "Rabbi, who sinned: this man or his parents, causing him to be born blind?"

Jesus said, "You're asking the wrong question. You're looking for someone to blame. There is no such cause-effect here. Look instead for what God can do. We need to be energetically at work for the One who sent me here, working while the sun shines. When night falls, the workday is over. For as long as I am the light in the world, there is plenty of light. I am the world's light."

He said this and then spit in the dust, made a clay paste with the saliva, rubbed the paste on the blind man's eyes, and said, "Go, wash at the Pool of Siloam" (Siloam means "Sent"). The man went away and washed—and saw.

Soon the town was buzzing. His relatives and those who year after year had seen him as a blind man begging, were saying, "Why, isn't this the man we knew, who sat here and begged?"

Others said, "It's him all right!"

But others objected, "It's not the same man at all. It just looks like him."

He said, "It's me, the very one."

They said, "How did your eyes get opened?"

"A man named Jesus made a paste and rubbed it on my eyes and told me, 'Go to Siloam and wash.' I did what he said. When I washed, I saw."

"So where is he?"

"I don't know." . . .

[The Pharisees continued to question the man. They even questioned his parents. But they were not satisfied with what they heard. They said the healed man was nothing but dirt and threw him into the street!]

Jesus heard that they had thrown him out, and went and found him. He asked him, "Do you believe in the Son of Man?"

The man said, "Point him out to me, sir, so that I can believe in him."

Jesus said, "You're looking right at him. Don't you recognize my voice?"

"Master, I believe," the man said, and worshiped him.

Jesus then said, "I came into the world to bring everything into the clear light of day, making all the distinctions clear, so that those who have never seen will see, and those who have made a great pretense of seeing will be exposed as blind."

Some of the Pharisees overheard him and said, "Does that mean you're calling us blind?"

Jesus said, "If you were really blind, you would be blameless, but since you claim to see everything so well, you're accountable for every fault and failure."

—John 9:1-12, 35-41 (*The Message*) ·

1. What one word or phrase stands out to you in the passage?

2. Why do you think the disciples asked the question, "Rabbi, who sinned: this man or his parents?"

3. Does our own wrongdoing ever cause an illness or other problem? Explain.

4. Give some examples of how we might make a false connection between our (bad) behavior and our illness or other difficulty.

5. What can you learn from this story about Christ's response to suffering in the world? What is the message for us today in this story?

Case Study: Caught in the Middle

John was seven when his parents divorced. He lived with his mom but was able to see his dad quite often. His mom did her best to keep things in his life as "normal" as possible. So that they could continue to live in the same nice house, she began working full-time, earning enough money to cover the monthly house payments. Both parents continued to take John on trips and supported him at his school programs and baseball games. John spent about one weekend a month with his dad.

John is fifteen now. He feels he needs and wants to be with his dad more often. His dad is willing to spend time letting him drive and he's enjoying the time with him more and more. He's able to talk more easily with his dad about guy stuff.

John's dad has remarried, and John gets along well with his stepmother and his two younger stepbrothers. They play basketball on the driveway and go away on weekend camping trips. Last weekend John asked his dad if he could come and live with him until he graduates. His dad was willing to explore the possibilities. However, John felt awkward approaching his mom about this, so he asked his dad to come over and talk it over together.

The meeting was friendly but awkward. John's dad made a good case for John's moving in with him and his family, but his mom mostly listened and didn't say much. "I don't know why your father wants to do this to me," she said. "He has his own family now. Why does he want you to live with him?"

That's when John told her it was his idea. "I still love you, Mom," John said, "and I really appreciate everything you've done for me, believe me. It's not like I won't be seeing you or anything like that. I'll come over. We'll still do stuff together. Things won't change that much. I just want to stay with dad and his family for a while."

But John's mom warned him that the move would have a long-lasting effect on their relationship. "Don't you know how lonely I'll be without you around the house?" she said. "Besides, I've worked all these years so we could have a nice place to live. And now you want to leave and go stay with your dad. I just don't understand."

John was frustrated. He didn't want to hurt his mother's feelings, and at the same time he really wanted to spend more time with his dad. He really didn't know what to do. He felt caught in the middle.

- What reasons would John have to stay with his mom?

- What reasons would John have to move in with his dad?

- What would you advise John to do? Why?

Brandon's Mess

There was once a dad who had a three-year-old son named Brandon.

One day Brandon sees his dad eating chocolate chip cookies in the living room and says to himself, *Daddy loves chocolate chip cookies with milk. So I'm going to give Daddy a glass of milk.* With that thought Brandon goes into the dining room and drags a chair from the dining room into the kitchen, leaving a trail of scratch marks on the floor.

Brandon climbs up on the chair and hitches himself onto the counter to pull at the cabinet door. Wham! It smashes against the adjacent cabinet door, leaving a gash where the handle hit it. Brandon reaches for a glass, accidentally knocking two others off the shelf, Crash! Tinkle, tinkle! But Brandon doesn't care. He's thinking, *I'm going to get Daddy some milk.*

Meanwhile, Brandon's dad is watching all this, wondering if he should step in and save the rest of his kitchen. He decides, for the moment, to watch a little more as Brandon scrambles off the chair, dodging the pieces of broken glass, and heads for the refrigerator.

Pulling violently on the refrigerator door, Brandon flings it wide open—and it stays open, of course. Brandon puts the glass on the floor—out of harm's way, supposedly—and grabs, not the little half gallon of milk, but the big gallon container that is full of milk. He rips it open, pours it in the vicinity of the glass, and even manages to get some milk in the glass. The rest goes all over the floor.

Finally done, Brandon puts the milk carton on the floor and picks up the glass, yelling, "Daddy, got something for you!" He runs into the living room, trips, and spills milk all over the place—the floor, the sofa, his dad.

Brandon stands up and looks around. He sees broken glass, milk everywhere, cabinets open, his dad with milk from his eyebrows to his toes, and starts to cry. Through his tears, he looks up at his dad with that pained expression that says, What are you going to do to me?

His dad only smiles. He doesn't see a kid that just destroyed his house. Instead he sees a beautiful little boy whom he loves very much. It doesn't matter what he's done. Brandon's dad stretches his arms out to hold his little boy tight and says, "This is my son!"

The Bible on Death and Dying

Working with one or more others,

1. Read your passage out loud.

2. Decide together on one key idea your assigned verses conveys about death and dying.

3. Find a creative way to express that idea to the rest of the group. Some possibilities:

- make a poster
- act it out or pantomime it
- write a slogan
- create a thirty-second radio or TV commercial
- create a "freeze frame" picture
- use your own idea

You may at some point in your presentation read all or part of your passage to the group.

Group 1: Genesis 3:1-6; Romans 5:12

- Key idea about death and dying: _____

_____

Group 2: Ecclesiastes 3:1-4; John 11:32-37

- Key idea about death and dying:_____

_____

Group 3: John 3:16; John 14:1-4; 1 Corinthians 15:55-57

- Key idea about death and dying:_____

_____

Group 4: Deuteronomy 31:8; Psalm 23:4

- Key idea about death and dying:_____

_____

Myths of Grief Inventory

Mark each of the following items as either "true" or "false." Don't try to guess what you think might be the "right" answer— respond as candidly and honestly as you can in terms of what you presently think about the grief process.

_____ 1. When someone you love has died, time will eventually allow you to get over your grief.

_____ 2. Having someone you care about die suddenly (as in a car accident) is far harder to deal with than having a loved one die as a result of a long-term illness.

_____ 3. After the death of someone you love, you should try not to think too much about the loss. In that way the painful feelings can slowly ease away.

_____ 4. You should think only about the positive side of your relationship with your deceased loved one; since he or she is no longer here, it would be disloyal to recall the negative aspects of your relationship.

_____ 5. You will eventually begin to feel better if you try to appear to be happy (even if you feel awful) and accept social invitations (even if you don't feel like it).

_____ 6. You can resolve old remaining conflicts that existed with the person who died, even though you can no longer talk together.

_____ 7. Having fun or laughing while in the grieving process may indicate that you really no longer feel hurt or miss the person who died.

_____ 8. Men should try to keep their emotions in check and really should not weep in public or otherwise openly show their grief over the death of someone they love.

_____ 9. After you've lost someone you love, your happiness with never be as complete as it was before—but you do have wonderful memories to provide comfort.

_____ 10. If you had a happy and fulfilling life prior to the loss of your loved one, you will likely be happy again in the next phase of your life.

—This survey is adapted from a workshop conducted by Dr. Susan J. Zonnebelt-Smeenge and Dr. Robert C. DeVries, © 1999, and is used with their permission.

A Guide for Difficult Conversations About Dying and Death

(for families)

This handout is meant for you to use with your parents and your older brothers and sisters. Please consider taking a half hour or so to talk over these important issues with them.

Caring for each other when we are faced with issues of death and dying is often emotionally and physically demanding. When families face the long-term care of a dying member, they often make decisions that reflect their own denial instead of the desires of the dying family member. And unexpected deaths in a family can plunge the family into emotional chaos.

Death and dying are not easy issues to discuss. But families who make time to talk about these things *before* they happen are usually better equipped to face the challenges and to respond in confidence that they are honoring one another's wishes.

Children should know how to access information about their parents' will. They should talk with parents about a living will and funeral arrangements.

Start by talking about these questions with your parents and older family members:

- How do you feel about talking about the issues of dying and death?

- What have been your experiences with dying and death?
- Do you have any fears about your own death?
- What is the best way to respond to persons who have experienced a death in their family?

Facing key issues about death and dying can help us live more confidently and overcome our fears and worries.

Here are three key areas to talk about with your family:

WILL

- Have your parents provided clear instructions regarding property and guardianship of minor children through a legal will in case something were to happen to them?
- Who is the person responsible to see that these wishes are followed through?
- What should you know about this information?

LIVING WILL AND ADVANCED DIRECTIVES

- Do your parents have a living will, or have they completed a list of advanced directives that should be followed if they were incapacitated in an accident? Where would you find a copy?

- Does their doctor have a clear understanding of the type of treatment they desire?
- Under what circumstances would you or family members ever want to be on life support?
- Do your parents ever wish to have a feeding tube?
- Do they want Hospice care?
- Are you and your family members registered organ donors?
- Where would you find important medical information if you had to provide it for someone regarding your parents' health history and/or medication?
- Under what circumstances would you or other family members want an autopsy? (For example, only if a doctor suggested that the information gained might benefit other family members? Or if the cause of death was not clear?)

FUNERAL PLANNING

- Have your parents made decisions regarding the type of funeral they desire to celebrate their life?
- Will they be cremated?
- Should there be a time for viewing with family and friends?
- Should the casket be open at the viewing?
- Should the service be at the church?
- How would they design the service to best represent their life and commitments?
- Are there important Scripture passages, hymns, readings that should be part of the service?

ADDITIONAL QUESTIONS AND ACTIVITIES

Ask the following questions of yourself as well as of your parents and other family members who are old enough to consider them.

1. Consider writing your own obituaries and sharing them with each other. Often as we reflect on how we would want to be remembered, we learn how we should be living our lives today.

2. If you were to develop a terminal illness, reflect on how you would want to spend time with your family and friends. What could make this meaningful to you and to them? (Special trips, a designated family time each week/month, phone calls, a party, renewing your marriage vows, making a special family album, a final family photo, and so on.)

3. What will be your legacy when you die? What values do you hope to pass on to others? What life lessons have you learned? What hopes do you have for your loved ones?

4. Consider writing thank-you notes to people who have already made a difference in your life. Thank them for specific ways they've helped you.

5. How does your Christian faith affect your views on life and death?

6. Is there any ritual or ceremony you'd like others to consider after your death as a way to remember and celebrate your relationship? (An annual trip to the cottage, planting a tree in your honor, and so forth.)

7. Read some books about death or rent some videos that explore the dynamics of dying people.

8. Think about the questions in this handout. Which ones seem awkward or uncomfortable to discuss? Why do you react this way? Is there fear involved in thinking about death and dying?

WILL

Case Study:

Dealing with Tragedy

On Tuesday, November 2, 1993, my life changed. My father committed suicide.

I was a junior in high school and had just arrived home from school. Soon my mother arrived home, followed by the senior pastor of my church. They explained that he (the pastor) had received a letter from my dad, indicating that he was going to kill himself. The letter gave no details.

When my siblings came home a few minutes later, my mother was meeting with a police officer who had come to file a missing persons report. While we huddled in the next room, there was a knock on the door. A county sheriff officer was standing at the door. We heard my mother scream, and we all knew that what we feared was true. My father had driven his car into a tree and was dead.

The hours and days that followed are some-what of a blur. A lot of people gathered at the house to support us. I remember thinking to myself that none of this had really happened; it couldn't be possible. I remember being surrounded by people who loved me and were willing to just be present. I am grateful for friends and family who just sat with us in silence, for tears and laughter, for others who brought meals. We even had a friend who brought toilet paper to the house! She said she couldn't think of anything else to do. When tragedy hits, people often say, "Call me if I can do anything." Sometimes it's better if you just do something practical, like bring toilet paper.

As a family we decided not to hide the truth of what really happened by saying, " Dad died of a heart attack," or, "Dad died in a car accident." Suicide is often the hidden secret of a family that gets buried in denial. Too many people are paralyzed for a lifetime of grief when they feel unable to share the truth. While it caused some people to shy away, I am grateful for those persons who allowed me to talk about my dad. Even my best friend found it too difficult to discuss and in time drifted away. I was fortunate to have others who embraced me and the memory of my father. About six months after my dad's suicide, a friend of mine had a dream about my dad. She wrote it all down and sent it to me. It is important for friends of people who experience tragedy in their lives to initiate these conversations. Opportunities like this to experience peo-ple's friendship and love in very meaningful ways have allowed me to heal.

We also found creative ways as a family to grieve and remember my dad. For the past seven years, we have all gathered on November 2 for dinner. My mother has asked each year if we want to continue this ritual. At least for now, it's part of what we need to do to remember. We also burn a candle at Christmas time in honor of my dad. At our church we place flowers in memory of him each year. Our church family's continued support and care has been very important to us.

I never blamed God for what happened, and I never stopped believing in God. God's love was present in and through the midst of our crisis—through others. It came in the form of hugs, casseroles, stories, and prayers. I sometimes asked myself why God allowed my dad to do this to himself. I wondered why my dad was never able to share his deepest fears with me (or others), because he was always so willing to share in my personal struggles. The letter he left behind made it clear that he loved us. My mother and the family therapist we saw for grief counseling stressed that we were in no way responsible for my father's choices.

What I continue to learn from my experience with tragedy and loss is that God redeems a broken world. God has allowed my family to heal over time. What could have been a detriment to our lives, drew us closer together. I've learned a lot about who I am. I strive to understand and embrace the human side of life that is filled with goodness but always is in need of God's grace for the things in life we can't understand. I learned the importance of reaching out for help, and I have decided to commit my life to a ministry of helping others.

Today I am happily married and pursuing my call in ministry. My family is doing well. We survived our loss.

Note: At the time of this writing, Edie Lenz is a seminarian at Western Theological Seminary.

Bible Study: Hope, Help, and Healing

As you work your way through this handout with your small group, please have different group members read the comments aloud to the group. Stop when you come to one of the following symbols and follow the directions:

 Talk over with your group.

 Go around the circle and have everyone respond.

 Jot down your personal, private response.

It's possible, even probable, that you will not graduate from high school without facing a sudden crisis or tragedy: an accident seriously injures a family member; a classmate is shot while working at a local convenience store; a good friend drowns in a boating accident; a tornado causes enormous damage and loss of life in your town. If you are fortunate enough not to have encountered a tragedy like this, you may well have a close friend who will need your help. While we can never be "ready" for such unwelcome events in our lives, it does help to equip ourselves with a basic understanding of the hope, help, and healing promised by God in the Bible.

1. DON'T BLAME YOURSELF

Far too many people blame themselves for the tragic deaths of others. They live burdened by irrational guilt. For example:

- Adam feels responsible for his father's cancer. He should have put more pressure on him to quit smoking.
- Scott thinks he should have stopped by his sister's house the day before because, if he had, she may not have committed suicide.
- Bethany feels she should have warned her sister not to go out with this guy who raped her.

Sometimes, of course, we do know the cause of certain tragedies. For example, suppose your neighbor drives while drunk and kills a pedestrian crossing the street. Or suppose you smoke a pack a day and end up with lung cancer. Far more often, though, we really don't know why bad things happen—why, for example, an earthquake kills hundreds, a drought starves thousands, a stray bullet kills an innocent child, someone's mom gets cancer, thousands die in a terrorist attack. All we can say is that bad things like this happen because we live in a sinful, imperfect world.

Jesus' disciples once asked him if a certain man was born blind because he had sinned or because his parents had sinned. "Neither this man nor his parents sinned," Jesus said, "but this happened that the work of God might be displayed in his life" (John 9:1-3). The disciples were asking the wrong question. They were looking for blame. The message for us today is that God is present when we suffer, and God's desire is for us to be whole, physically and spiritually. Even as Jesus restored the sight of the blind man, so he can also provide spiritual wholeness to all who confess him as Lord.

What kind of tragedies hit you hardest and make you wonder why in the world these things happen?

 What's one area of your life where you tend to blame yourself when it's not really your fault?

2. SEEK HELP FROM OTHERS

Don't suffer in silence.

"Two are better than one. . . . If one falls down, his friend can help him up. . . . A cord of three strands is not quickly broken" (Eccles. 4:9-10, 12).

 What do these verses say about seeking help?

 Why do some people who face tragic losses not talk with anyone or ask for help?

 Give an example of a time when someone helped you through a difficult time or when you wish someone had offered to help.

3. HANG ON TO HOPE

Most people get through the traumatic losses in their life and learn to live productive and happy lives. They move beyond the pain and blame to a place where they can reinvest in their own life with purpose and meaning.

 Share what gives you hope when you have to go through a crisis or tragedy. If you wish, you can refer to a passage from the Bible or something you believe about God.

 What are possible responses to someone who claims they have lost their faith because of the event of a tragic loss in their life?

4. REMEMBER THAT GOD LOVES YOU

People who have lost a close friend or family member to suicide or a tragic accident often struggle with their relationship with God. Unfortunately they spend a lot of their time blaming God instead of being comforted by God. Remember that God desires to walk beside you and to be present to you. God wants to walk you through the valley of hurt and disappointment. God weeps with you in your tragedy and wants to be a source of comfort and healing.

 Jot down a time when you questioned whether God really cared.

 How have you experienced God's comfort in your life?

5. BE THERE FOR OTHERS

Everyone loves to share good times with his or her friends. Believe it or not, though, sometimes when people face the most difficult moments of their lives, they feel abandoned by those who are closest to them. Sometimes this results from personal isolation that may be caused by depression. At other times it is because their friends are afraid of not saying the right thing, so they say nothing at all. God calls us to a *ministry of presence* with hurting people. To walk alongside them. To be there.

Read 2 Corinthians 1:3-11.

 What does Paul suggest we do for others?

 Can you remember a time when someone practiced the "ministry of presence" with you? What did they do that was reassuring to you?

 How can we be present in the life of those who suffer tragic losses?

—Adapted from *The Word on Family* by Jim Burns, ©1997, Gospel Light/Regal Books, Ventura, CA 93003. Used by permission.

WHY ME? WHEN LIFE'S NOT FAIR
Evaluation Form

How would you describe your group sessions?

- [ ] interesting
- [ ] boring
- [ ] related to my daily life
- [ ] unrelated to my daily life
- [ ] dominated by leader
- [ ] good group participation, discussion

Which activities did you like best?

- [ ] small group activity
- [ ] discussing with the whole group
- [ ] reading/studying the Bible
- [ ] using the handouts
- [ ] prayer time
- [ ] other:

_____

_____

_____

What did you gain from this course?

- [ ] a clearer idea of what a biblical world-view is
- [ ] a way to make better sense of the things that happen to me
- [ ] a stronger sense of the brokenness and the goodness of creation
- [ ] a sense that I have something to contribute to the restoration of God's world
- [ ] I'm learning to encourage others to grow spiritually

In general, how would you rate this course?

- [ ] excellent
- [ ] good
- [ ] fair
- [ ] poor

If you could change anything about this course, what would it be? Please comment and add anything else that's on your mind:

_____

_____

_____

_____

_____

_____

_____

_____

Name (optional):

_____

Age or school grade:

_____

Male or female:

_____

Church:

_____

City/State/Province:

_____

Please send completed form to

Faith Alive
2850 Kalamazoo Avenue SE
Grand Rapids, MI 49560

Thanks!

Leader Evaluation Form

BACKGROUND

Size of group:
☐ under 5
☐ 5-10
☐ 10-15
☐ over 15

School grade of participants:
☐ grade 10
☐ grade 11
☐ grade 12
☐ post-high

Length of group sessions:
☐ under 30 minutes
☐ 30-45 minutes
☐ 45-60 minutes
☐ over 60 minutes

Please check items that describe you:
☐ male
☐ female
☐ ordained or professional church staff
☐ elder or deacon
☐ professional teacher
☐ church school or catechism teacher
  (three or more years)
☐ youth group leader

HANDOUTS FOR GROUP MEMBERS

In general, I
☐ did not use the handouts
☐ used the handouts frequently

Please check items that describe the handouts:
☐ too few
☐ too many
☐ helpful
☐ not helpful

MEETING GUIDES AND GROUP PROCESS

Please check the items that describe the activities suggested for each group session:
☐ varied
☐ monotonous
☐ creative
☐ dull
☐ clear
☐ unclear
☐ interesting to participants
☐ uninteresting to participants
☐ too many
☐ too few

Please check the items that describe the Theme Thoughts provided in the meeting guides:
☐ helpful, stimulating
☐ not helpful or stimulating
☐ overly complex, long
☐ about right level of difficulty
☐ clear
☐ unclear

The course in general was true to the Reformed/Presbyterian tradition.
☐ agree
☐ disagree
☐ not sure

Please check those procedures that worked best for you:
☐ small group discussions
☐ whole group discussions
☐ handouts
☐ use of session options
☐ other (please write in)

_____

_____

_____

_____

_____

Please check the items that describe the group sessions:

☐ lively
☐ dull
☐ dominated by leader
☐ involved most participants
☐ relevant to lives of participants
☐ irrelevant to lives of participants
☐ worthwhile
☐ not worthwhile

In general I would rate this material as

☐ excellent
☐ good
☐ fair
☐ poor

Additional comments on any aspect of this program:

Name (optional)

Church

City/State/Province

Please send completed form to

Faith Alive
2850 Kalamazoo Ave. SE
Grand Rapids, Michigan 49560

Thank you!